Song & Dread

ALSO BY OTONIYA J. OKOT BITEK

100 Days

A Is for Acholi

Song & Dread

Poems

Otoniya J. Okot Bitek

WITH A FOREWORD BY PETER MIDGLEY

Talonbooks

Talonbooks
9259 Shaughnessy Street, Vancouver, British Columbia, Canada v6p 6r4
talonbooks.com

Talonbooks is located on xʷməθkʷəy̓əm, Sḵwx̱wú7mesh, and səl̓ilwətaʔɬ Lands.

First printing: 2023

Typeset in Jenson
Printed and bound in Canada on 100% post-consumer recycled paper

Interior and cover design by Typesmith
Cover artwork: *Mapping the Everyday* by Beth W. Stewart

Talonbooks acknowledges the financial support of the Canada Council for the Arts, the Government of Canada through the Canada Book Fund, and the Province of British Columbia through the British Columbia Arts Council and the Book Publishing Tax Credit.

Canadä   Canada Council   Conseil des arts   BRITISH   BRITISH COLUMBIA
           for the Arts   du Canada   COLUMBIA   ARTS COUNCIL
                                                           An agency of the Province of British Columbia

Library and Archives Canada Cataloguing in Publication

Title: Song & dread : poems / Otoniya J. Okot Bitek ;
with a foreword by Peter Midgley.
Other titles: Song and dread
Names: Okot Bitek, Otoniya J., author. | Midgley, Peter, 1965- writer of foreword.
Identifiers: Canadiana 20220451605 | ISBN 9781772015164 (softcover)
Classification: LCC PS8629.K68 S56 2023 | DDC c811/.6—dc23

for those that we lost and for us who survived

Foreword

by Peter Midgley

The distance around the edge of any circle is a little more than three times the distance across it: this is the simplest explanation of the mathematical constant pi, which we commonly represent as 3.14... That decimal spirals on. Mathematicians have reached 62.8 trillion digits but have yet to find a recurring pattern.

Otoniya Okot Bitek started writing these poems on March 14 – Pi Day. The first series of poems in *Song & Dread* – a set of fifty pi day poems – recounts the days of horror through repetition. Where her earlier collection, *100 Days*, was a response to the one hundred days of the Rwandan genocide, here she considers a different killer: COVID-19 ("this thing," she calls it). *Song & Dread* is a searingly honest response to the pandemic. We remain struck by the ever increasing number of deaths, and by the futility of these deaths: the repetition, the repetitiveness. But most of all, as we read *Song & Dread*, we are struck by the author's ability to make sense of the ordinary amid the extraordinary.

As an adjective, the word "constant" refers to nonvariance – the repetition of the deaths as a result of "this thing." In this sense, in these poems, "constant" means not depending on some variable; not changing as the variables change. But what is "constant" in mathematics depends on the context: a constant in a narrower context could be regarded as a variable in a broader one. Whose death is noted, for example, is a constant within the larger variable of deaths: we do not readily notice the Black people who died of "this thing" at rates nearly double their share of the population.

The poems in *Song & Dread* careen between a broader focus on the world at large and the narrower focus of what it means to be Black in this world. Mathematicians may continue to search for a recurring pattern in pi, but these poems reveal the constants and recurrences within the context of "this thing." So do the silences that surround Black people's deaths. To read Otoniya Okot Bitek's poetry is to be ever vigilant; with the merest tilt of her pen, she disrupts the constants of this world, gives them new contexts. She probes and she pushes, never allowing the reader a moment to relax and just consume her words.

The words sneak up on you: in "pi day 44" we read that "protesters protest / the right to work / because / work makes you free." And then, in the deluge of words that is "breadcrumbs," we encounter the phrase: "Arbeit macht frei." COVID, camps, and history collapse into one dreadful constant.

In the deluge of words in poems like "breadcrumbs," we find hidden the stories that no one listened for: a recurrence, a constant. The names of those who died on the periphery are pulled out of news stories and internet links and placed in front of us. The poem appears to be just another wall of text, but it combines every aspect of what we've dealt with in the collection, and in the pandemic: a deluge of information, race, class, indifference, blindness. *Song & Dread* grows incrementally around these words and themes, spiralling out like the decimals of pi: job insecurity, labour, the exploitation of fossil fuels, colonialism, travel bans, who is vulnerable. The only constancy amid uncertainty is that life goes on. Pi: the contextually variable constant.

When the deluge of words in "pi day 44" or "breadcrumbs" hits you, wordslettersinformation overwhelmsyouandthe linkstomoreinformation stifle all meaning – except the names of those who lied buried under these words of indifference: Sharon Roberts, Belly Mujinga, Errol Graham … these poems name them. Otoniya gives them names, memorializes them, gives them a visibility they never had in life.

What remains unsaid, but is important to remember, is that Sharon Roberts is Black. For much of the world, Black is not important. But in "pi day 48," and in this entire collection, Black is central. The horror of the repetition is terrifying, and the echoes of upper-middle-class terror and fragility are palpable throughout. Long-term care has been compromised by Sharon Roberts's absence, and that is news. But for Sharon Roberts, the labourer in the facility that gave her "this thing," there is no care. That is not news. With every repetition we are reminded who's labour and who's class. Who matters and who doesn't.

And that's the heart of it. It invariably comes down to race and class and gender, no matter how we try to pretend otherwise. These are the things that remain constant, recur: who has and who hasn't; who matters and who doesn't. In Song & Dread, we discover the limits of our compassion – and how those limits correspond with race and class.

The poems in the pi series build to a stormy, angry

crescendo, and then, after the pouring rains, we get the gentle love poems, the poems about domesticity and belonging. The constants that ground us in a troubled world. These are lullabies appended to the end of a tumultuous time, but we wait for the explosion we know with certainty will come. And it comes, oh it comes as the poet cries out: "let us not arouse the dead." Throughout *Song & Dread*, Otoniya Okot Bitek has roused the dead. Hush now. Let them speak. *Listen* ...

SONG

&

DREAD

song & dread

sometimes there's song & sometimes there's dread
sometimes an awfulness thick as lava crawls up the wall
sometimes there's gratitude & other times not
sometimes the dreariness punctuates & levitates
sometimes there's glory in the wearer of the tunic
sometimes a halo or a cloud
sometimes there's music there

pi day 1

march 14 2020

here we are straddling the yet
because
after this
we can't reclaim innocence
after this
there won't be comfort in not knowing

pi day 2

white panels of the wall at shell with the yellow strip
the splash of red
this morning the gas price
falls
falls
on the way back home
falls
another two cents

this morning we're thinking about this benefit
this morning we also remember when gas prices were less
than a dollar
this morning we also remember when ken saro-wiwa was
still alive

pi day 3

on the third day the battering begins in earnest

first up
normalize is the demand normalize

at the grocery store
toïlet paper shelves remain in the clear

the healers remind us to
flatten flatten flatten the curve

& here we are
with potatoes in our hands

pi day 4

at the health centre buddy with a mask on
wants a letter that clears him to fly
wants to be tested

the healthcare worker tells him she cannot give him such a letter
but he's been in isolation for two weeks & has no symptoms
yes she says but he could have since gotten infected locally
so she can't get him tested because he has no symptoms

anyway
she gets him a letter stating that he has no symptoms
that should work
he thanks her
folds the letter carefully
places it in his backpack
thanks he says from behind his mask

pi day 5

sometimes i think about
the never-ending chorus of crickets

sometimes i think about
the single cricket at the beach last year
obnoxious in its singular song

today at a meeting
i ask how full-time regular faculty
might support
non-regular faculty
who can be given thirty days' notice &
therefore not get paid in the summertime
when the projections
are that there might not be much work
since international
students with their exorbitant school fees
will not be let into the country
because of the
you know
travel ban for all foreigners

except americans
one colleague suggests that we discuss this

crickets

pi day 6

as i was brushing my hair today
i remember the story about
hair as a vector in spreading the virus
about some people in wuhan
thinking about shaving off beards
about how we used to have our hair shaved off
as a sign of mourning

pi day 7

a dentist's office still taking new patients
a barber shop still doing business stylist unmasked
the massage therapist shop with a sign out that says

in order to protect our employees
if you have travelled in the last fourteen days
please stay away
and come back later

pi day 8

six days since i wore earrings
but the garbage was picked up
the gardens outside are still manicured
& cherry blossoms are outrageous in their fullness

pi day 9

we keep saying that these are extraordinary days
extraordinary
extra beyond ordinary
extra beyond the mundane
extra like toronto
extra extra extra extra etc etc etc

but nature doesn't seem to reflect that

pi day 10

today the sky is a stupid blue
a garish blue a rude blue
i forget that it's only a backdrop
to budding & flowering trees

today the professoriate is less firm
about the importance of finishing off the term
along with administration
the professors profess
the above-neck need to assess
to judge to pass to fail
to maintain rigour rigour rigour

also from the professoriate
the call for martyrdom
the claims of anxiety
the need to be seen to be doing everything they can
for our students

pi day 11

this is what we don't have to remember

     the claim that black people don't get the virus
     the claim that the viruses don't like heat
     the claim that grandparents would be willing to die
        for the economy
     that the cure being worse than the problem is a
        function of letting

the difference between releasing a character & casting one
is the path of icarus determined by his father
or by himself

pi day 12

three days of lockdown
& two more pieces of anxiety to add

come into the house take off all your clothes
& put them into a plastic bag
& straight into the wash

if physical money may be a vector
then where can i get the coins
for the building washing machine that i've avoided

pi day 13

last night weighted footnotes
drag me through sleep

footnotes as foundational
as creep as notice board
as conversation dump
as traditional hefty

like this morning the account of the black woman in britain
whose husband was told that she was not a priority
& she died she died she died from this thing

now him still at home with his diabetes & her body
like a footnote

pi day 14

today an impossibly bent-over tree seeks my eye

skeletal branches budding this is the season
deep yellow forsythia this is the season
bluish-grey white cherry blossoms this is the season
large pink magnolia petals like tongues against the sky
this also is the season
this is the season

there has been a before
& there will be an after
with or without us
on these lands

pi day 15

someone heard that her mother's sister caught the thing
she's not expected to survive
this one lost her father last month her husband is in hospital
she's keeping the thing company by herself at home
& that one was touch & go for a while
but she's home now

pi day 16

now they're calling it the feminist virus
because it kills more men than it does women
because the uk *metro* headline announces
      woman with family locked down in italy
      poses naked with face masks to urge
      everyone to be safe

another woman dreams of her family some dead
some alive some she may never see again

somewhere somewhere a group of women
are in a factory producing 50k masks a day in lockdown
& the cbc news clip ends with
      they care more for patriotism
      than for their own families

pi day 17

& so the roll call begins
the unending cough of the neighbour
who smokes everyday right under our bedroom window
the screams of a man echoing off the empty primary school
    walls a block away
the cat diagnosed with something like the thing possibly
    from the owner
the tear-gassing & beating by who have been termed the
    beasts of mombasa
the tens of thousands of workers needed to pick fruit in
    britain within two weeks
patient cam from rwanda
in which a dancer moves
to jerusalema
by master kg
featuring nomcebo

thing is
for all the joy in the dance of this patient
the lyrics are a prayer
yet all we read from the video is the lightness of his steps

pi day 18

when witnesses line up
to account & recount
& accounts build to explain & contextualize
the un-precedented-ness of this thing

in living memory we have come through
& come through
& come through
& come through
& come through

but they only listen to themselves

pi day 19

the tide is out today & so the skies are big big big across
the mountains snow-capped or not sit confident in their
    mass-dom
behind the mountains castles & castles of cloud
masses of them
light & dark
soft & ominous
grey & startlingly white
the mountains are a playscape beneath the clouds today

pi day 20

how long will we have to live like this
asks a tweeterer

also an echo
from days before this
moments
articulations of other desperations

what is the crucial point
that disperses this question from everybody's mouth

pi day 21

navels begin to creep upwards
towards the sternum

most people won't notice
because they're drawn to the numbers on the screen
because they're stupefied by the facts
because they've left the solid of their bodies
& now they leave no footprints
& cast no shadows either

pi day 22

two days ago a train engineer in la
drove his train at full speed
intending to crash it into the usns *mercy*

you only get this chance once he said
the whole world is watching he said
i had to he said
people don't know what's going on he said
the engineer was charged with
one
count
of train wrecking

pi day 23

french doctors jean-paul mira & camille locht
assert that a probable vaccine for this thing
should first be tested in africa

but for rouge hermès
a collection dedicated to the beauty of the lip
beauty is a gesture
says the hermès canada collection

soccer players didier drogba samuel eto'o & demba ba
do not appreciate the gesture
from the doctors' lips

pi day 24

hero defined
as singular　　　those whose bravery matters
plural　　　　　those for whom everyday acts are perceived as
　　　　　　　　　courageous
also plural　　　those who do the work we rather don't
　　　　　　　　those for whom a $2 raise is sufficient hazard pay
　　　　　　　　those without whom the city starves
　　　　　　　　those without whom the garbage is not picked up
　　　　　　　　liquor stores
　　　　　　　　shut tight transit will not run
　　　　　　　　those for whom we beat pots in the evening
　　　　　　　　those for whom we shout play music clap
　　　　　　　　those whom we meekly obey at the grocery stores
　　　　　　　　as they yell at us not to move to the next yellow
　　　　　　　　line until we have been directed to do so
　　　　　　　　those who allow us to stay home stay safe stay away
　　　　　　　　from this thing
　　　　　　　　against which not all employers can
　　　　　　　　or will provide protection

　　　　　　　　because we deserve to stay alive
　　　　　　　　& they deserve the hero worship
　　　　　　　　& we need heroes now more than ever

archaic for hero　　　who are youthful
　　　　　　　　　　muscular
　　　　　　　　　　& wear capes

pi day 25

i've been wearing the same four sets of clothing
for almost a month
some for days on end
with no washing in between
every day had become a sluggish mess

today the colour in my closet is in riot
& the jewelry is a long scream

this thing will not stop me from
this shiny ring

pi day 26

some things remain consistent
a man polishes his car
on the next block two landscapers
with leaf blowers
a perfectly clean road

the maserati parked by the side of the house

the blue sky still elicits a gasp
the child hates its mother
retaliation bullying & threats
remain currency on the world stage

pi day 27

four new deaths yesterday
new deaths
deaths as a new
as news
four brand new
as good
four deaths as good news as relief

all sixty-one dresses worn by villanelle
from *killing eve*

a styling show
given the attention to style

a killing show given the deadly villanelle
a style of poetry

nineteen lines with quatrains
& other fancy words
that i don't care to learn or use

the most famous villanelle
is dylan thomas's rage rage
how do we rage when four deaths in one day is
a good news night

pi day 28

some thought that sports commentators might be out of work

    general trend from united nations
    us & uk is
    still more deaths every day than the last
    japan joins the death track chart
    now italy
    now us has cut straight through italy's curve
    & is on course for highest death toll globally
    within five days
    australia still looking promising
    uk still parallel to italy
    indian infections picking up speed after slow early pace
    number of cases in spain surpasses 150,000 mark

commentators find a new sport

pi day 29

headline
      uk pm boris johnson
      having led the anti-immigrant brexit campaign
      is being treated in a hospital system
      where eight uk doctors who have died
      from corona virus were all immigrants

headline
      uk corona virus live
      boris johnson continues to improve
      death toll rises in england
      scotland & wales

headline
      downing street says
      uk prime minister is "in good spirits"
      after third night in intensive care

headline
      doctor who warned boris johnson
      about ppe
      dies
      after contracting corona virus

quote from said uk prime minister
      more families
      many more families
      are going to lose loved ones
      before their time

pi day 30

for all the giants falling
& the unreported lonesome deaths
& already forgotten
      slipped out from fast-growing charts & curves
& lost lost lost in ever reaching numbers

all the songs that will remain unsung
after we lost the music

bill withers
manu dibango
john prine
wallace roney
ellis marsalis
...

a child rides his bike in a quiet construction site
look ma no hands
his mother sees him

pi day 31

the isolation of the two quarantined foreign nationals
the big apple pays prisoners $6 an hour

to dig graves

planking is the shape of a curve
not exercise
not a flat piece of wood

burundi is still a country protected by god

pi day 32

a woman says
it would be a shame to stay at home
& let the government tell you what to do

not everyone drank the kool-aid
the man alongside her says
look at all the people he says
here for a march against tyranny he says
to show the world he says
that we're not okay with unlawful lockdowns
& quarantines he says
not everyone drank the kool-aid
he says again
on another lovely day in vancouver

pi day 33

listen

in fallowfield manchester
a policeman threatens a man with pepper spray
arrests & handcuffs him
as he drops off food to vulnerable family

in new york
a woman loses her husband
& only child
within three days to this thing

in washington
a president claims
complete authority

listen
the policeman says
you'll be next

we're far enough inside this thing to remember when it was
passed on through travel we're also far enough in to recall days
when it was clear that travellers were vectors it wasn't that long
before it became clear that local transmission was a thing &
then nursing homes & then crowd restrictions first five hundred
then fifty & then clusters & then daily updates by politicians
& top doctors & graphs that read exponentially & figures that
parsed out local & international transmission & then border
shutdowns & interprovincial shutdowns & finally lockdown

so the authorities in guangzhou count as we do local &
international transmissions & of the one hundred & eleven
africans tested nineteen were imported cases the report states
& having largely stamped out in-country transmission of the
coronavirus authorities are worried that one of the biggest risks
of a second wave in the epidemic stems from infected people
coming from abroad the report further states in the meantime
just to be safe a video shared on social media focuses on a notice
taken from a mcdonald's restaurant in guangzhou

> we've been informed that from now on black people are
> not allowed to enter the restaurant

the restaurant has apologized stating that the ban on
black people was not representative of our inclusive values
immediately upon learning of an unauthorized communication
to our guests at a restaurant in guangzhou we immediately
closed the restaurant the restaurant added that it had conducted
diversity and inclusion training in the branch

pi day 35

first was the roll call for the musicians
& as melodies died
the pipers & the horns began their awful call
filmmakers
poets
photographers
designers
novelists
artists
mothers
brothers
siblings
niblings
sisters
fathers

in the morning may we wake up to tomorrow's fog
or join the roll

pi day 36

      for the rich
      a dilemma
the headline says
whether to quarantine with staff or do their own chores

the article begins with an anecdote from the head of a
private staffing agency
who gets a call from a client who needs help
on how to change a vacuum bag & where in the house
to find a spare the rest of the article is hidden behind the
paywall of the *wall street journal*

~~only the rich can appreciate their own dilemmas~~

pi day 37

the well of words is dry
sense making an act of imagination
imagination to process understanding
there's a moment a turn a shift
a coming to know
a new way of nothing
an empty volta

pi day 38

a princess wears expensive clothes while volunteering
& here's where you can buy them

a church spire might not get rebuilt after all
& here's why

a gunman kills sixteen people
& here's where

everything is easy
everything is better
everything is normal
everything is available in the link below

pi day 39

yesterday i forgot to take my daily pill
so i dredged the internet for advice
the internet said
      do this four more days
      & you will suffer catastrophic weight loss

as if i could ever be as small as i feel inside

today as i take my pill
the internet says
a hundred & eighty-three thousand lives
are now lost to this thing

a handful of sand wet with ocean water
specks of sand as lives

to illustrate the drama
of millions of lives
many as small as mine
snuffed snuffed snuffed

the ocean licks the sand
rhythmically & patiently
unmoved

pi day 40

first read
       if we can't manage with our ventilators
       & our healthcare systems
       & our wealth
       & our progressive ways of being
       how will they manage

inside this nightmare
where hundreds dying daily &
graphs ever steeping
the saviours roll out plans
to save africa

the salivation now a waterfall
a curse
& now fingers at the ready
waiting for africans to die
so that the headlines bear out the story they want

pi day 41

in the daylight
the floor isn't threatening
except in the headlines where the world crashes

& in the sidewalks cracked in the night
by the slow & powerful growth
of trees seeking liberation

pi day 42

empty grocery shelves	class terror
undone nails	class terror
cash transactions	class terror
unstyled hair	class terror
unwashed clothing	class terror
unavailable yeast	class terror
class terror	class terror
closed parks	class terror
sunny days spent inside	class terror

in the evening wild cheers & the banging of pots & pans
come daytime a doctor who's stopped from in-person
banking because he's a healthcare worker

pi day 43

thin days
skinny days
days so light they sit on your eyelashes for a moment

blink

& with that blink
all those stories

pi day 44

protesters protest
the right to work
because
work makes you free

home	left american anti-lockdown protester
explore	right auschwitz camp gate
notifications	photo
messages	side by side memory making
bookmarks	photo
lists	chicago auschwitz
profile	photo
more	present memory ache
tweet	bounding echo

pi day·45

last night with stone in hand
me & first rat locked in an eye embrace
i throw the stone at it
i miss
i walk across pick up the stone & throw it again
i miss again
first rat walks across to the stone
picks it up & brings it to me

another rat
an older rat
first rat shakes its head so we both watch
older rat limps away
with a shorter left leg

slowly with stone firmly in hand i aim for & meet
the back of first rat
& crush it
our eyes still locked

as i release my grip on the stone
& feel the bound of first rat
fanged out eyes wide open
aim at my neck

pi day 46

i miss my own self
i miss the weight of my head in my hand
& the weightlessness when i walk
beside my own self

i miss the pleasure of cool water
fresh of good cold beer
instant heat of the sun on skin
coffee-shop coffee
even the rude whirr of the espresso maker

i miss writing a poem for its own self
for its own need to be in the world

she stopped work last monday at a toronto long-term-care
centre by friday she died at home alone she stopped work
last monday at a toronto long-term-care centre by friday
she died at home alone she stopped work last monday at a
toronto long-term-care centre by friday she died at home
alone she stopped work last monday at a toronto long-term-
care centre by friday she died at home alone she stopped
work last monday at a toronto long-term-care centre by
friday she died at home alone she stopped work last monday
at a toronto long-term-care centre by friday she died at
home alone she stopped work last monday at a toronto
long-term-care centre by friday she died at home alone she
died at home alone she died at home alone she died at home
alone she died at home alone she died at home alone she
died at home alone she died at home alone she died at home
alone she died at home alone she died at home alone she
died at home alone she died at home alone is probably the
only thing most of us will ever know about sharon roberts a
personal support worker at the downsview long-term-care
centre who died of this thing in toronto on the first of may

pi day 48

needing prayer
kneeding prayer
kneading prayer

pi day 49

spat on coughed at by someone who said they had this thing
spat on coughed at along with her workmate
by someone who said they had this thing

spat on coughed at by someone who said they had this thing
& ended up sick with this thing

ended up in hospital & got intubated because she was
spat on coughed at by someone who said they had this thing
& then

      statements of regret
      & serious questions about her death
      & recognition for the loss of another of our frontline
         workers

an admission that she was vulnerable
& that perhaps she should have been stood down
from the frontline

there were announcements of goodwill
a letter to ask for the extension of the compensation scheme
to belly mujinga's family & other transportation workers
who die of this thing

      absolutely heartbreaking
      nobody should be spat at
      any allegation is taken very seriously
      all claims will be investigated

this is a criminal matter
& not about having more protective equipment

& what the prime minister has called tragic
is now yesterday's news

pi day 50

so she said follow me
follow me
follow the names
follow me
follow the dance
follow me she said

tap tap
ta tap tap
ta tap tap
ta tap tap tap

follow me she said follow me
tap tap ta tap tap ta tap tap tap
tap tap ta tap tap ta tap tap tap
follow me she said

today is no day to die

breadcrumbs

p i d a y 2 6 donaldtrumpthreatenstocutfundingforthewh
ohttpswwwftcomcontent193453e3479f4fef9234d0f9f14c
5a6efinancialtimessubscribetounlockthiscontentpaywall
httpswwwcnncomvideosworld20200408whodefendscor
onavirusresponsetrumpcriticismvpxcnn p i d a y 2 7 https
wwwtheringercomtv20204821212957killingevevillanelle
outfitsrankedrankingeverysingleoutfitwornbyvillanelleo
nkillingeverankedtheringer p i d a y 2 9 eightukdoctorsdi
edfromcoronavirusyou'vereachedyourlimitoffreearticles
alreadyasubscriberloginnewyorktimespaywallhttpswww
theguardiancompoliticslive2020apr09ukcoronaviruslive
lockdownextendedborisjohnsoninhospitalcovid19latestu
pdatesborisjohnsonleavesintensivecareasraabwarnsofno
earlyendtolockdownasithappenedthisarticleismorethant
woyearsoldsupportclimatejournalismtheworldcantwaitt
heguardianhttpswwwmirrorcouknewsuknewsbreakingd
octorwhowarnedboris21840465doctorwhowarnedborisj
ohnsonaboutppediesaftercontractingcoronavirusdrabdu
lchowdhury53warnedprimeministerborisjohnsonthatfro
ntlineworkersdesperatelyneededmoreppethemirror
p i d a y 3 0 httpswwwrollingstonecommusicmusiccountr
yjohnprineobit253684johnprineoneofamericasgreatestso
ngwritersdeadat73rollingstone p i d a y 3 1 httpswwwtheg
uardiancomusnews2020apr10newyorkcoronavirusinequ
alitydividetwocitiescmpshareiosappother p i d a y 3 1 atal
eoftwonewyorkspandemiclaysbareacitysshockinginequit
iestheguardianthecoronavirushaslaidbaretwosocietiesdiv
idedonlinesofclassandraceadividereflectedinskeweddeat
hfigureshttpswwwaacomtrenafricaburundiconfirmsfirst

2covid19cases1787083burundiconfirmsfirst2covid19case
sburundianswhoarrivedfromrwandadubaitestpositivean
adoluagency **p i d a y 3 2** httpstwittercomdandickspftstat
us1249449767404363776protesttoendthelocdownhapp
eningnowinvancouver#endthelockdowntwitter530pmap
ril122020 **p i d a y 3 3** httpswwwtheguardiancomuknews2
020apr11uklockdownpoliceapologiseaftermanthreatened
withpepperspraythisarticleismorethan2yearsolduklockd
ownpoliceapologiseaftermanthreatenedwithpepperspray
theincidentinfallowfieldmachesterwasfilmedbyneighbou
rssupportclimatejournalismtheworldcantwaittheguardia
n **p i d a y 3 4** httpswwwtheguardiancomuknews2020apr1
1uklockdownpoliceapologiseaftermanthreatenedwithpep
perspraychinamcdonaldsapologisesforguangzhoubanpnb
lackpeople14april2020mcdonaldsinchinahasapologiseda
fterabranchintheindustrialcityofguangzhoubarredblackp
eoplefromenteringbbcnewshttpswwwcbccanewsworldch
inaafricacoronavirus15531335chinadeniesdiscriminationa
gainstafricansinrecentwaveofcovid19caseschinadismisses
allegationsafteranecdotalreportsofdiscriminationtargtin
gpersonsofcolourthomsonreutersposterapril142020821p
mhttpstravelnoirecomafricannationalsfacingdiscriminat
ioninchinaafricansinchinaforciblyevicted&homelessduet
odiscriminationafricachinanewstravelnoire **p i d a y 3 6** h
ttpswwwwsjcomarticlesfortherichadilemmaquarantinew
ithstaffordotheirownchores11587051916fortherichadilem
maquaratinewithstaffordotheirownchoressomewealthyh
omeownersareselfisolatingwithstaffduringthecoronaviru
spandemicwhileothersarecookingcleaningandtakingoutt
heirowntrashcontinuereadingyourarticlewithawsjmemb
ershipviewmembershipoptionspaywallthewallstretjourn
al **p i d a y 3 8** httpscastyleyahoocommeghanmarklejames

persepantsstansmithsneakers002451208htmlguccounter
1meghanmarklewears$410sweatpantswhilevolunteeringi
nlahereswhereyoucanbuythemyahoo!lifeapril1820202mi
nreadmeaghanmarklehasbeenspottedvolunteeringinlaov
erthepastfewdayshttpswwwtimesofisraelcomayearafterb
lazenotredamerestorationhaltedbyvirusayearaftercatastr
ophicblazenotredamerestorationhaltedbyvirusfailuretor
emove250tonsofdamagedscaffoldingatsitethreatensfurth
erharmstolandmarkmacronstillhopefulofhavingcathedra
lreopenfor2024parisolympics20april2020thetimesofisre
alhttpswwwaljazeeracomnews202004gunmankills16nov
ascotiacanadaworstmassshooting200420005904903htm
lgunmankills18innovascotiaincanadasdeadliestshootingp
olicesaygunman51yearoldgabrielwortmanappearedatone
stagetohavebeenwearingpartofapoliceunifrom16killedinc
anadasworstmassshootingindecadesaljazeera20april2020
p i d a y 4 0 httpstimecom5816299coronavirusafricaventi
latorsdoctorsfewdoctorsfewerventilatorsafricacountriest
heyaredefenselessagainstinevitablespreadofcoronavirus7
daysale!subscribefor99churryofferends103april72020911
amedttimehttpswwwbloombergcomnewsarticles202004
17virusseenkilling300000inafricaevenwithinterventions
viruscouldkill300000inafricaevenwithinterventionsgove
rnmentsresponseswillaffecttrajectorypandemiccouldpush
29millionpeopleintoextremepovertyapril172020300ame
dtupdaterapril182020at400amedtbloomberg p i d a y 4 1
httpsglobalnewscanews6878115novascotiashootingkiller
historydisputes/novascotiagunmanwasinvolvedinseveral
disputesbeforeshootingrcmpsayspostedapril282020532p
mwedliketoshowyounotificationsforthelatestnewsfeatur
esandupdatesnothanksallowglobalnewshttpswwwstraigh
tcomfinancegaspricesplummetinmetrovancouvergaspric

esplummetinmetrovancouvertheinternationalglutinoilsu
ppliesisofferingabreaktomotoristsinthelowermainlandan
dthefraservalleythepricehasfallento79.9centsperlitreint
woeastvancouvergasstationsapril272020tsubscribetoour
notficationsforthelatestnewsandupdatesyoucandisablean
ytimelatersubsrcibethegeorgiastraight p i d a y 4 2 httpsw
wwcbccanewscanadatorontodoctortdbankcovid19155470
10itsaslapinthefacetorontodoctorsayshewastoldhecanten
twelocaltdbranchtdsaysscreeningquestionsdontincludea
skingifsomeoneisahealtchcareworkeratorontodoctorsays
hesveryconcernedabouttdbankscovid19policiesafterhesa
yshewasntallowedtoenterhislocalbranchsimplybecauseh
esahealthcareworkercbcnewsapr282020 p i d a y 4 3 https
wwwtheguardiancomsociety2020may01manwhostarveda
fterbenefitscutoffhadpulledoutownteethmanwhostarved
afterbenefitscutoffhadpulledoutownteethfamilyprovides
detailsoferrolgrahamsfataldeclineaspartofactionagainstd
wperrolgrahama57yearoldgrandfatherwhodiedofstarvati
onwhenhisbenefitswerecutoffhadbecomesomentallyillth
athisfamilybelievehepulledouthisownteethwithpliersthe
yhaverevealedfri1may20200700thisarticleismorethan2ye
arsoldsupportclimatejournalismtheworldcantwaityouver
ead6artcilesinthelastyear p i d a y 4 4 httpstwittercomDe
nnisKosuthstatus1256309653455003648ref_srctwsrc5Et
fw7Ctwcamp5Etweetembed7Ctwterm5E1256309653455
0036487Ctwgr5E65e9ff47c3427721bbc0ebf9d345a6393e
611e977Ctwcon5Es1&refurlhttps3A2F2Fwwwbusinessin
sidercom2Fauschwitzarbeitmachtfreiantilockdownposte
ratchicagorally20205agerestrictedadultcontentthisconte
ntmightnotbeappropriateforeveryonetoviewthismediayo
ullneedtoaddyourbirthdaytoyourprofiletwitteralsousesy
ouragetoshowmorerelevantcontentincludingadsasexplai

nedinourprivacypolicylearnmoreifthisphotbothersyoujo
ineffortstobetterourworlifyouhaventalreadymay22020h
ereitisinmotionforthosewhoquestioifitwasrealmay32020
p i d a y 4 5 httpswwwnewsweekcomkkkhoodsupermarke
tsanteesandiegomaskscoronavirus150170ifbclidiwar2fw5
p43lj8zqk6hhbztwwvhbloxe7uijhzpo3nranlhifszrkxokw
aavosandiegomanwearskkkhoodtosipermarketaftercoun
tyorderspublictowearfacemasksofficialshavecondemned
amanincaliforniawhowaspicturedwearingamakeshiftkluk
luxklanhoodwhileshoppingatasupermarketlistentothisar
ticlenow5420at351amedtnewsweek **p i d a y 4 7** httpsww
wlatimescomlifestylestory20200506lacoronaviruslesson
spostquarantinethechangeswehopearepermanentonceth
epandemicisovertheresnosugarcoatingitthecoronavirusp
andemicalongwiththeunprecedentedmeasuresbeingtaken
toslowitsspreadhaveupendedourlivesaffectedourliveliho
odsandprofoundlyalteredthelokkandfeelofourcommunit
iesinonceunimaginablewayslimitedtimeoffer$1for6mont
hsmay62020730amptlosangelestimes **p i d a y 4 8** httpsw
wwthestarcomnewsgta20200505shestoppedworklastmo
ndayatatorontolongtermcarecentrebyfridayshediedatho
mealonehtmlutmsourcefacebookutmmediumsocialmedia
utmcampaigngtautmcontentcoviddeathfrontlineshestop
pedworklastmondayatatorontolongtermcarecentrebyfrid
ayshediedathomealonefor24yearssharonrobertsworkedw
ithseniorsatthedownsviewlongtermcarecentrecoworkers
aresharingworriesaboutgownsmasksandotherpoliciestue
may52020whennewsbreaksdontmissitgetfreebreakingne
wsalertsandmoreinyourbrowserfromthestaryesmaybelat
erforunlimitedaccesstothetorontostarforonly$99weekca
ncelanytimeunlocknowpaywalltorontostar **p i d a y 4 8** ht
tpsnaacporgcoronavirusfightwithfactsweallhavequestion

sandconcernsaswenavigatethispandemicgettheimformat
ionyouneedtoprotectyourselfandyourcommunityhealthd
isparitiesleftblackamericansvulnerabletocontractingcovi
d19anddyingfromitathigherratesnearlytwotimesthanthei
rshareofthepopulation**p i d a y 4 9** httpswwwtheguardian
comworld2020may13policeexaminecctvfootageofsuspect
whospatatukrailworkerwholaterdiedpoliceexaminecctvf
ootageofasuspectwhospatataukrailworkerwholaterdiedc
oronavirusdeathofticketofficercomesamidreportsofkeyw
orkersbeingspatatandcoughedatondutythisarticleismore
than2yearsoldwen13may2020bstpolicehavediscoveredcct
vfootageofasuspctwhospatatarailwayticketofficeworkerw
holaterdiedofcoronavirusamidfearsthatspittingisbeingus
edasaweaponagainstfrontlineworkerssupporttheguardia
navailabelforeveryonefundedbyreaderscontributesubscri
betheguardianhttpswwwbbccomnewsukenglandlondon5
261607icoronavirusvictoriaticketworkerdiesafterbeingsp
atat12may2020arailwayticketofficeworkerhasdiedwithco
ronavirusafterbeingspatatbyamanwhoclaimedhehadcovi
d19bellymujinga47whohadunderlyingrespiratoryproble
mswasworkingatvictoriastatioinlondoninmarchwhenshe
wasassualtedalongwithafemalecolleaguewithindaysofthe
incidentbothwomenfellillwiththevirusnewsyoucantrusti
snewsyoucanuseregisterforabbccounttoday12may2020
bbcnews

FINEPRINTS

oh

to be a single[1] sheet[2] of paper[3]

beneath
a wri[4]ti[5]n[6]g hand

~~m~~
a
~~r~~
k

~~me[7] write all[8] over me[9]~~

---

1   aggravation contained on a page
2   & control like history is zero nothing else in this notebook but lines & lines
3   bare walls   naked floor   text   a clear past to nowhere
4   oh   to be a single sheet of paper beneath your writing hand
5   mark me   crush this line of control
6   note formula   note me   note my name
7   write   write   write madly
8   write   because three times three makes nine
9   & i think i might know from where i come

before & after this city

1. there's a dead a dread a bed full of monsters
   a led tongue a lead tongue a church an address
   at one church square a bear now dead now dread
   now led away away away into a circus a red ball
   a trapeze artist at one church square a dog a log
   many logs many many logs a forest a cathedral
   now gone a dread again a dread again a dread

2. i have an address at the cathedral at one church
   square a song a long echo back & forward there's
   a bell a fryer's bell a sonic echo a back & forward
   in time a guitar with no broken string a bowl of water
   a man walks across the street in front of the church
   at one church square

3. i have an abandonment a gig a lid a bid
    for mercy for time for sequence
    for prayer for hair for a kiss for an umbrella a
    man walks back & forward in time in front
    of the church at one church square there's a dog
    a dread a bell a church fryer a bowl full of mercy
    a gig a haircut a sign assign assign a sigh for
    the guitar with no songs left to bear

4. i have a bear a lair a friar a prayer at
    one church square a cathedral a booth
    a shadow an echo a woman with an armful
    of plaits a mercy a god a god a god who
    won't listen but can bear to know to blow
    to flow to grow to bear any grace with
    a mandolin a guitar with no songs left
    a bowl full of sighs a dog a god a red ball
    an echo a sign with an address at the cathedral
    at one church square

5. i have a kiss a bliss a line of colour across
    the room an abandonment a scaffolding a
    determination a category a map a canopy
    a bit of stained glass at the cathedral before
    the church at one church square a plea
    to acknowledge the bear the seed the light
    the air the friar the lair the haircut the kiss
    for the barber the dog the log the log the log
    the forest the plea for support to cease to stop

6. i have a clue a view a blue a due date
   a reckoning a pronoun that holds us
   together as due for a haircut a scaffolding
   a resonance a metal bar a room of posies
   & posers & dozers a red bell an umbrella
   a bowl full of roses & prayer & care &
   fare thee well my lady fare thee well gain &
   back & forward in time

7. i have a church at one church square where
   the bottom has fallen out & a tub made from
   concrete holds artists in prayer at the fair with
   a bear with a red nose & a trapeze artist a kiss
   a blissful afternoon a booth a guitar with
   no songs left amazed amazed amazed

8. i have a pestilence a penitence a flagellation
   a condemnation a moat a float a boat a coat
   a red ball a fryer's bells a church at one church
   square a cathedral a shadow a woman with
   an armful of plaits a dare a flare a care
   a clarinet with a broken reed a bowl full
   of prayer & flowers & song

9. i have a determination a red metal bar
   a condemnation at the cathedral at one
   church square a wisdom a glint a flint
   a dint of mercy a man walking back
   & forward in time a reservation a call
   a prayer a warning to cease a tall stack
   of smoke on a cold day some rain a kiss
   for the barber a haircut a bell a dog
   a bear a prayer a situation

10. i have a doll a moll a stall where the haircuts
    are taking place in front of one church square
    with blue metal spokes a pink flag & yellow
    bars of plastic to make patterns make love
    make love make pitches to the dodgers &
    posers & dozers who counter the wisdom
    by signing up for a haircut & kisses for the
    barber & misses for the song full of bowls
    of roses & bears & stares from passersby

11. i have a mercy for the cathedral at one church
square a flair a care a dare for flower power
for prayer for a dog a god a log a log many logs
a forest long gone with the bear to the circus
& the red ball & the red trapeze & the
man walking forward & back in front
of the church in the evening among kisses
for the barber as a song floats in the water
of a concrete bath

when the instructions are given for jericho

we line up
we of the margins
to sing & pray like everyone else
but they point at us
us infidel
& tell us go

so now we've fallen into story
& inside story is all there is
further & further
out from the wall
of jericho

a golden god awaits
but this is all there is this is all there is
this is all there is
but this is what we hear

not you infidel
not you with your infidelity
not you
not you

we head for ethiopia

i to look for anu
you for aoife of the marvellous thighs

away from the margins
& the walls

us in a darkness
with hard edges & a soft centre

we forget about jericho
because we have each other
& a cabin that waits

we fall
we fall
we fall
& then flight

but today we wake up

both of us barrel-chested
we look at each other
& laugh & laugh & laugh

funny that both of us
have lost all evidence of youth
we laugh until we ache

& then it becomes clear
that our belly muscles
that the ones that used to hurt
from laughter
have now relaxed
opened

& now we have more space for grief
& now we know each other
as containments for much more

& there's a manifesto knocking at the door

so we swear to dismember language
we pinky-promise to make a list

first we'll take english apart
word by inept word
we'll begin with articles
& chop them up with the sword
on the mantle

this is all there is

this is all there is

this is all there is this
is all there is this is
all there is
this becoming
is what they wanted us to be
us coming into flight

this is all there is

& now you're on your knees

caught
muttering   muttering
religion like a tulip
sprouts from your head
the way it does
                on tuesdays

you're on your knees
your hands over your face

amen   amen   amen
your head pours out
starry nights
monkey shit

a snake slithers out from the side of your neck
god slithers

& now you're at the beach

a family in single file at the shore
the boy red shirt green pants   cartwheels
women   heavy with a multitude of colour   shuffle
three girls red dresses gold trim   skip skip skipping
a man an orange shirt   rolled-up pants   at the rear
a riot of colour against the blue-grey of the sea & sky
they stop to picnic
& colour takes a break

it's thursday morning

a gong from the night sky
the rest of the world is asleep
& you're madly collecting thirty words
& their kin

words slip from your fingers
stick to your sleeves
slide back slide back gravity-bound

you're going to have to recreate the whole world
with language from these thirty words
but what's language without possession
or colour

thursday 4 a.m.

thirteen words left
none of them articles
none of them adjectives
none of them pronouns
none of them colour
not even black

a list of things to do
a pile of letters sixty-seven long
a blank calendar

words fall from your mouth
in cascade

then you
you like the shiver of a spider's web in the sun

we're on the top floor of the four-faced liar

christ & the   devil in deep conversation
fineprinting   the two of them
fineprinting   the laws of devotion
fineprinting   the meaning of sin

shandon explodes in a warm glow

you're pointing at the stars & me at you

like stars we're made of nothing
like stars we're headed to nothing
but this the most sublime of moments

is this what it means to be a star

this is our fondest path yet
you at the stars
& me at you pointing at the stars
evolution & revolution

you're complete
you said this morning
you're complete
but we're flaming out   we're flaming out

is this what it is to belong
in the country of stars

this is my day off

having already
lost a beautiful string of lettering
that had formed into a poem
i should take the day off

these days
lost poems remain lost
a requiem is the best that i can do

you & i on the couch

you in your work clothes
& i in my bathrobe
both of us cloaked
in the silence of this morning

we've got a list of words to go through

laundry
banking
insistence
baking
insouciance
moment
distinctions
slithery
computational
wave songs
universality
dispersal
& settling

do words feel the tongue of the speaker
in the middle of a dream

where broadway meets main
us pounding into each other
like dogs
each intent on becoming the other

from monday on   we swear everything will change
by saturday   we're waiting
to slide into things

what is a good day to die

distinctions

your loveliness   for this there is no struggle
your location on the east gate
no one is coming to acknowledge your presence
the relationship between a stiff breeze & a full skirt
there is nothing else

wave song

i'm riding a wave of hail marys & underneath a chorus
you're only human
you're only human
&
you're just a woman

deep baritones & alto currents
& the occasional soprano spray
you cannot move in just yet
you cannot move in just yet

i'm standing at the threshold
a river of hail marys rushes by
there's a tide i'm waiting for
clear spirits will carry me there

insistence

she walks at the edge of a ditch
with her arms outstretched
her mouth tight with focus

the edge of this ditch like the rest of it
is muddy
she slips
catches herself
but she will not walk on the path

that's for walkers
she says
that's for walkers
i'm not a walker
she says
i'm a balancer
i hold the world divided in my palms

from monday on

you suggest
that we bleed out the possessives
that nothing can belong to anyone or anything
share one   share alike

now there's no claim for darling

on friday

adjectives nouns & adverbs
in a bowl
like fruit
from last week
starting to go bad
starting to have the sick sweet smell
of fruit going bad
starting to die
starting to know that fruit knows
that they're dead
the moment that they're picked from the tree

a collection of wilting words
waiting to be thrown out
into the compost

by saturday

breakfast in bed for a tired woman
one day in the year   two   three
a bouquet of flowers
a lopsided smile
a sensuous pinch

ah bwana lakini wewe

let us not arouse the dead

Author's Note

Every March 14, I join folks around the world who celebrate Pi Day, or Pie Day, but in 2020, with the pall of COVID-19 over everything, it seemed like a good day to start documenting how the media, the fear, and lockdown came together in our lives. I was teaching; it was almost the end of term. Students would come to class and share the numbers and the stories from their home countries that would later be reflected in the media, or not. It seemed like what we heard on social media, on TV or radio, was only part of it, but we couldn't continue to gather in class. Shortly after, the lockdown followed and many of us were confined to our homes. But what else was going on while we were inside? What were we not being told? We wore double sets of gloves, joined carefully spaced lineups for over-priced masks and tried not to touch anything, especially not our faces. We all felt wrecked, didn't we? At the same time, we knew that there were some people for whom lockdown was not a choice and they were the ones we relied on for our food, supplies, and healthcare. For a while, we heard the daily cheer for healthcare workers and the colourful expressions of gratitude in shop windows and on banners everywhere. At the same time was the dismal roll call, every day, announcements were made, public health officials presented graphs and numbers and more countries revealed the fatalities within their nations. And then suddenly, it all seemed to switch from the conversation around controlling an illness we didn't know enough about to a conversation about political freedom and rights.

Among the offerings of that year was the boundless energy of thousands and thousands of young people in Nigeria demanding freedom and fairness from their government as they protested police brutality. I did not write about the #EndSARS protest movement, given the brutal response from the government – others have and will – but it remains among the few bright spots of that year. That, alongside birdsong and images of animals emerging into urban spaces, the crisp outline of the Himalayan mountains without polluted air, and the clear water in Venice.

Along with the Pi Day poems are poems about relation, relationship to words, and sliding into the abstract. Those poems were written shortly after I'd completed a long public collaboration during which I wrote the poems that would become *100 Days* (University of Alberta Press, 2016). In retrospect, I feel that those poems allowed me to look at the world again, without the weight of memorializing a genocide. Those now feel like my freedom poems and in this collection, I hope that they offer the reader a way out and a space towards a world that imagines all of us.

I'm so grateful to have had the privilege of time and safety for this poetic practice, a small space of sustenance for me.

Acknowledgments

Song & Dread is my littlest-sister title of poems, preceded by
100 Days and *A Is for Acholi*. All three are books about wit-
nessing. All three are also illustrations of the privilege that I
have been afforded to think and write and be published. First
thanks to those two titles for making way for *Song & Dread*.
Neither of them would have been published on the weight
of my poems alone and this book, too, is also a tremendous
work of encouragement, collaboration, friendship, and love.

I'm so grateful to Cecily Nicholson. Not just because she
edited this book and showed me how to think about these
poems, but because Cecily was the first Black woman poet I
came to know in Canada. As she signed my copy of her first
book, *Triage*, she wrote a note for me to continue to write
poetry. So I did. I have a deep admiration for Cecily for liv-
ing as a political commitment to a better life for all of us; for
poetic practice that is a witnessing, a gathering, a call to action,
documentation, beauty, artistry, generosity, and love.

Jenny Penberthy insisted that these poems needed to find
a home. Thank you for the faith in my work, Jenny, and for
your steadfast support and the gift of a first edition copy of
Song of Lawino that I keep close to my heart.

Thank you to Beth Stewart, whose lively and powerful
artwork features on the cover of *Song & Dread*.

Thank you, Catriona Strang, for your warm presence and
steady hand on this work.

Peter Midgley, thank you for saying yes, again, and for
your beautiful foreword.

I'm so appreciative of the support for all the people at Talonbooks. So many of my favourite writers have had their work come through Talon and I'm honoured to have this littlest sister among them.

In the spring of 2021, I spent time at the Deer Lake Artist Residency at Baldwin House in Burnaby, BC, as part of the Shadbolt Fellowship and Simon Fraser University Writer-in-Residence Program. I'm grateful for the time, space, and beauty I was accorded to see just how much poetry I had been writing.

Some of these poems have been printed elsewhere and I'm grateful to the following people for making space:

Bhakti Shringapure invited me to share some of the pi poems in *Warscapes* magazine as I was writing them. At the time, I was thinking about them as anti-memory poems. Early versions of "pi day 10," "pi day 14," "pi day 13," "pi day 1," "pi day 3," and "pi day 4" were published as part of the Corona Notebook Series on Warscapes.com.

Lyse Lemieux invited me to write two poems alongside her extraordinary solo exhibit *Painted Drawings* at WAAP in Vancouver (June 6 to July 20, 2019). The titular poem comes from a stanza from the commissioned poem, "Song and Dread."

The poems in the last section of this book originally appeared as a free e-book titled *Sublime: Lost Words* (The Elephants, 2018), with gratitude to the editor, Broc Rossell. Of these poems, "it's thursday morning" was published in *The Capilano Review* 3, no. 28 (Spring 2016), with gratitude to Andrea Actis.

Gratitude to Joni Low, who commissioned "before and after this city" for *What Are Our Supports* (December 2022), an incredible invitation to respond to the group projects of five artists at One Cathedral Square in Vancouver. The opportunity to respond to the work of artists, like Lyse Lemieux's (*Painted Drawings*) and this one at Cathedral Square, invites poetry as play, abstraction, and all kinds of possible. I really loved writing "before and after the city." ·

Thank you to the internet, for the privilege of access to retrieve the weblinks containing the stories from which many of the pi poems were inspired. These are acknowledged as "breadcrumbs."

I'm not sure that anyone wants to be named as the group of usual suspects, but Omer Aijazi, Chrissie Arnold, and Erin Baines were the first readers of these poems; we laughed so hard about a sinkful of kale in bleach water. I'm always grateful for friendship and love and the generosity of people who hold so much of my nonsense and still stick by me.

My friends at Decolonizing Cellulite know who they are.

Thank you to Pádhraic Ó Raghallaigh, for handing me a leather-bound book in the summer of 2014 and reminding me that after the *100 Days* poems, I could write the mundane, the sublime, and the fantastical.

Otoniya J. Okot Bitek is a poet and scholar. Her collection of poetry *100 Days* (University of Alberta Press, 2016) won the INDIEFAB Book of the Year Award for poetry and the Glenna Luschei Prize for African Poetry. She is an assistant professor of Black Studies at Queen's University, where she teaches and writes in the English and Gender Studies departments.

Photo: Seasmin Taylor